First published in Belgium and Holland by Clavis Uitgeverij, Hasselt – Amsterdam, 2009
Copyright © 2009, Clavis Uitgeverij

English translation from the Dutch by Clavis Publishing Inc. New York
Copyright © 2016 for the English language edition: Clavis Publishing Inc. New York

Visit us on the web at www.clavisbooks.com

Pilots and What They Do written by and illustrated by Liesbet Slegers
Original title: *De piloot*
Translated from the Dutch by Clavis Publishing

ISBN 978-1-60537-300-3

This book was printed in August 2016 at Publikum d.o.o., Slavka Rodica 6, Belgrade, Serbia

First Edition
10 9 8 7 6 5 4 3 2 1

Pilots
and What They Do

Liesbet Slegers

Clavis

NEW YORK

It's nice to visit a foreign country on holiday.

Some people go abroad for their jobs, too.

You can take the car or train to get there.

But isn't an airplane even better? Flying is really fast.

And it's very exciting to be so high above the clouds.

The pilot makes sure everyone arrives safely.

sunglasses

The pilot wears a uniform. He looks handsome, doesn't he?

The golden stripes on his coat show his rank:

the co-pilot has three stripes, while the captain has four stripes.

High in the sky, the sun shines through the large windows

at the front of the plane.

That's why the pilot needs his sunglasses.

Otherwise he will be blinded by the bright light!

He also carries his pilot's bag with him.

It contains all the maps he needs.

Girls as well as boys can become pilots, of course!

pilot's hat

tie

pilot's coat with stripes

pilot's trousers

pilot's bag

control column

The pilot sits in the cockpit to fly the airplane.

That's a little room in the very front of the plane

with a compass, an altimeter, a speed indicator, a fuel indicator….

During the flight the pilot has to keep a close eye on everything.

The control tower is in the middle of the airport.

The people who work there can see all the planes

on their screens and through the windows.

They tell the pilot which runway he can use over the radio.

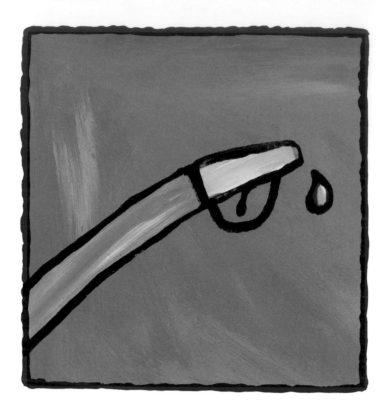

The airplane is waiting to leave.

Does it have enough fuel?

Are the engines all right?

Are the wings ready to go?

The pilot checks everything thoroughly, because he has to make sure the plane and the passengers will be safe!

The airplane is now ready to depart.

All the luggage is loaded into the cargo hold.

The captain is in charge of the airplane

and commands everyone who works there.

He is sitting in the cockpit with the co-pilot.

The flight attendants help the passengers to their seats.

Later on, they will bring them food and drinks.

But first they show them how to travel safely on a plane.

Everyone is on board.... Fasten your seatbelts!

The pilot is talking to the control tower over the radio.

The engines start and the plane carefully moves

to the right runway via the taxiway.

The people in the tower tell the pilot where to go,

because they know exactly where other planes will take off or land.

The plane has reached the runway.

It needs a head wind; otherwise it can't take off!

The tower tells the pilot he is allowed to take off.

How exiting! The brakes are released and the airplane goes really fast.

The pilot pulls the control column and the nose of the plane goes up.

The engines are turning at full speed. The plane takes off.

The wheels leave the ground and the wings are carried by the air,

like a bird....

The airplane is flying!

The wheels disappear into the belly of the airplane.

The plane goes higher and higher,

until it is completely above the clouds.

On the instrument panel, the pilot checks everything:

the height, the speed, the wind direction....

During the flight, the plane passes the control towers of other airports.

They keep the pilot informed and suggest another route

when a storm is coming, or when another plane is coming too close.

In the meantime, the pilot can enjoy the splendid views.
The clouds sparkle in the sunshine and when he looks down,
he can see the most amazing things: snow-covered mountains,
islands in the ocean, the lights of big cities at night…
during the entire flight.

When the plane reaches its destination,

the control tower tells the pilot which runway he can use.

Slowly, the pilot steers the plane to the ground,

pointing the nose down.

The wings expand as far as possible and the wheels appear again.

Soon the plane touches down on the ground! It has landed.

The engines slow down and the pilot brakes until the airplane

is standing still.

Everyone gets off the plane. It only takes a couple of hours to arrive
in a completely different country. That's amazing, isn't it?
The pilots and flight attendants go to a hotel to rest.
The captain fills out the paperwork and flight report.
Then they all get ready to fly to a new destination,
maybe a tropical island....

Pilots love flying more than anything. They think it's fantastic!
For them, nothing is better than feeling as free as a bird:
flying between and above the clouds, in the sunlight,
above the highest mountains, over deserts and oceans....

And you, what do you want to be when you grow up?
Maybe you dream about flying high in the sky too....